THE LITTLE BOOK OF
LIGHT CODES
WORKBOOK

LAARA

All Rights Reserved.
Copyright © 2024 by Jaclyn Herod
www.LightCodesByLaara.com

No part of this book may be reproduced or transmitted in any form or by any means, electronic or mechanical, including photocopying, recording, or by any information storage or retrieval system, without permission in writing from the publisher, except in case of brief quotations embodied in critical reviews and certain other noncommercial uses permitted by copyright law.

Publisher: Peacock Wisdom Publishing
ISBN (Paperback): 978-1-777351-57-1

Waiver: The author of this book does not dispense medical advice or other professional advice or prescribe the use of any technique as a form of diagnosis or treatment for any physical, emotional, or medical condition. The intent of the author is only to offer information of an anecdotal and general nature that may be part of your quest for emotional and spiritual wellbeing. If you or others use any of the information or other content in this book, the author and the publisher assume no responsibility for the direct or indirect consequences. The reader should consult his or her medical, health, or other professional before adopting any of the suggestions in this book or drawing inferences from it.

Contents

Introduction	1
Welcome	2
How to use this book	3

Symbols
Lakahana	8
Gamma	11
Yah'kma	15
Akahanama	19
Yah'tkh	23
Rugth	27
Scryb'th	31
Ahagma	35
Kh'mak	39
Turla	43
Tsuhami	47
Turmar	51
Teglih	55
Kahlsi	59
Hydahama	63
Bahan	67
Halahma	71
Khalagma	75
Hoitma	79
Dahanama	83
Go to Beauty and Peace	87
Pahma	91
Lahma	95
Henama	99
Aman'kh	103
Jamaka	107
Akuna	111
Yunami	115
Humbelah	119
Delight	123
Kahalula	127
Pahgyahma	131
Yahma	135
Hennami	139
Gyla	143
Kahli	147
Ughma	151
Suri	155
Commagt	159
Zahay'kma	163
Anami	167
The Love That You Are	171
Jyak'ma	175
Galagma	179
Tungah	183
Kalak'tuk	187
Lakama	191
Shizama	195
Jayagk	199
Panma	203
Kalimar	207
I Am Presence	211

Congratulations!	215

Introduction

Welcome

Welcome to *The Little Book of Light Codes Workbook*, a guided self-healing workbook designed to support you on your journey towards emotional well-being and personal growth. This workbook is more than just pages and prompts, it is a companion best used alongside your healing journey with *The Little Book of Light Codes* and *The Little Book of Light Codes Oracle Deck*. For optimal results and for more information on each symbol and the topics each symbol holds, be sure to grab a copy of the full book, *The Little Book of Light Codes,* available through bookstores worldwide.

In this workbook, you will find all 52 symbols from *The Little Book of Light Codes*, along with journaling prompts to assimilate the healing energies of each symbol. These beautiful pages are awaiting your creative expression and personal evolution! You are invited to express your thoughts and feelings through coloring and doodling, as well as through the thought-provoking self-exploration prompts. If you need more space to expand your process, move your answers into a separate journal, and allow your discovery to unfold!

As you use this workbook, please know that you are supported by the healing energies of the Universe, including Lady Isis and Jeshua, along with the powerful consciousness held by the Light Codes. There is no rush to move through this book. This workbook helps us reflect upon deep aspects of ourself that require bravery and honesty. This is deep work that you will hopefully receive many benefits from as you continue to evolve on your incredible path. Allow the journey to unfold in the timing that is appropriate and right for you. If you find yourself in need of additional support, please find a qualified professional to assist you. Take the time to find the right practitioner to support you in your unique situation, and know that you have an abundance of tools that can help you move into greater levels of peace. It's important to remember that healing and learning about ourselves is an intimate process, that begins with accepting who we are today, and celebrating that person! You are a powerful soul who has embarked on a lifetime of lessons, discovery, and experiences! Some of these are challenging, and some of them are delightful. Wherever you are today, whatever you are feeling and navigating, know that your soul has all of the capability to handle, heal, and excel.

We all wish you blessings and Love for your amazing and wonderful journey.

Laara

How to Use This Book

Set Your Intentions
Before you begin, take a moment to reflect on your intentions for using this workbook. What areas of your life do you want to focus on? Whether it's managing stress, improving relationships, or fostering self-love, clearly defining your goals will guide your journaling and healing experience.

Use the Light Codes
The Light Codes hold powerful energies, healings, and wisdom for you to work with consciously and subconsciously. Explore gazing upon the Light Code after reading the prompts for the day, then compare your response after working with the Light Code. Notice if there's a difference, and then let it go.

Consistency is Key
Commit to a regular practice with the Light Codes. Set aside a few moments each day or week to engage with the prompts and reflect on your experiences. Consistency will deepen your connection with yourself and enhance the effectiveness of your process.

Honesty and Openness
This workbook is a safe space for your thoughts and feelings. Be honest with yourself as you respond to the prompts. Embrace vulnerability and allow the pages to capture your authentic journey.

Honesty and Openness

This workbook is a safe space for your thoughts and feelings. Be honest with yourself as you respond to the prompts. Embrace vulnerability and allow the pages to capture your authentic journey.

Progress Tracking

Use the designated spaces to track your progress and celebrate victories—big or small. Reflecting on your journey will reinforce positive habits and inspire continued growth.

Be Creative

You are incouraged to use these pages to express your innermost thoughts, feelings, and discoveries. Be creative! Use colors, doodle, and have fun discovering more about who you are and who you came here to be!

Remember

Your journey is unique, and so is your healing process. This workbook is a tool to guide you, but the power lies within you. Embrace each entry as a step toward self-discovery and healing. As you move through this experience, may you find solace, clarity, and the strength to nurture the most important relationship of all—the one with yourself.

Working with the Light Codes

Everyone has their own unique experience while working with Light Codes. The energies an individual needs, their sensitivity level, and their conscious or unconscious connection with the Codes will determine each user's experience. Some people feel sensations, others may "see" energies (such as perceiving shapes or lights in their mind's eye). Others may notice a different thought or memory, and some might receive nothing at all! Be the sacred witness of your own experience, remaining free of judgment, holding your intentions for the best outcome.

As a baseline practice for working with Light Codes, use the Grounding Practice Meditation provided below, to help you become present, grounded, relaxed, and open to receive the messages and energies on a conscious level. If your favorite meditations bring you into a grounded state, use those instead. As with all things, the more conscious we are, the more connected and empowered we are, and the more meditation expands our conscious mind and helps us tap into the collective unconscious. That said, Light Codes work with us for our highest good, whether or not we are aware of them.

Grounding Practice

Sit in a chair with your feet flat on the floor. Relax. Breathe. On each inhale, imagine your feet are suction cups, pulling energy up from the earth. On each exhale, relax. With each inhale, imagine your feet drawing energy up from Gaia, through the floor, into your legs. Feel the energy moving up in your body with each in-breath until it reaches the top of your head. Release it out of the top of your head (through your crown chakra). Imagine the energy flowing up and out like water cascading from a fountain.

Practice this grounding exercise often, so it becomes second nature. Using this process at the beginning of any meditation practice will help center you and prepare you to enter any level of awareness you may wish to access. Grounding connects your heart and mind. It can promote wellness, improve sleep, lower your blood pressure, and reduce stress and anxiety. It's a great way to start and end each day!

When you are ready, with your eyes open, gaze upon the Code. Feel its energy. Try to remain open to the various ways the Light Code can speak to you. You may feel sensations or perceive light, or thoughts may pop into your mind. Stay with the Light Code for as long as is comfortable. When you are done, thank the Code for its help. Use this symbol as often as you feel is right for you.

"To have access to your heart is to have access to your soul."

~ LAARA

"Light Codes are Life Codes"

As you begin your journey with Light Codes, Lakahana offers gentle guidance on a beautiful path of self-discovery. This symbol offers encouragement as you release fears, walking away from false and limiting beliefs, and slowly open yourself up to Love.

REFLECT ON ANY FALSE BELIEFS THAT MAY BE INFLUENCING YOUR PERCEPTION OF SELF AND THE WORLD. WHAT LAYERS OF MISCONCEPTION OR LIMITING BELIEFS HAVE YOU IDENTIFIED?

_____
_____
_____
_____

CONTEMPLATE THE IDEA OF HEALING WITH A SENSE OF LIGHTNESS. HOW CAN YOU APPROACH YOUR HEALING JOURNEY WITH A LIGHTER, MORE COMPASSIONATE PERSPECTIVE?

_____
_____
_____
_____

WEEKLY PROGRESS / NOTABLE EXPERIENCES

Gamma

Opening Channels of Light, Connecting to Source,
Breaking Through, Dissolving Barriers

Gamma brings joy and reminds us to view situations from another perspective, make a different choice, or find a new solution. Shedding light on something reveals a different outlook, and almost every situation holds a positive intent.

REFLECT ON YOUR CURRENT SITUATION OR STRUGGLE. HOW ARE YOU CURRENTLY VIEWING IT? WHAT EMOTIONS OR THOUGHTS ARE PREDOMINANT?

CONTEMPLATE THE NOTION THAT THERE MAY BE ANOTHER CHOICE YOU CAN MAKE IN YOUR CURRENT CIRCUMSTANCES. WHAT ALTERNATIVE CHOICES COME TO MIND?

HOW CAN YOU REMAIN OPEN AND RECEPTIVE TO POTENTIAL SOLUTIONS? WHAT STEPS CAN YOU TAKE TO ACTIVELY SEEK AND RECOGNIZE NEW POSSIBILITIES IN YOUR SITUATION?

HOW CAN YOU BRING MORE LIGHT TO YOUR CURRENT CHALLENGES?

- [ ] _____
- [ ] _____
- [ ] _____
- [ ] _____
- [ ] _____
- [ ] _____
- [ ] _____

WHAT PRACTICES OR ACTIVITIES BRING YOU JOY AND HOW CAN YOU ADD THEM EVERYDAY?

- [ ] _____
- [ ] _____
- [ ] _____
- [ ] _____
- [ ] _____
- [ ] _____
- [ ] _____

"Love is to be found, even in the darkest places."

~LAARA

WEEKLY PROGRESS / NOTABLE EXPERIENCES

Create a healing space at home to support inner healing. Yah'kma's energy helps move from suffering to a nurturing, supportive, and Light-filled existence.

REFLECT ON WHAT A SACRED HEALING SPACE MEANS TO YOU. WHAT ELEMENTS OR FEATURES WOULD YOU INCLUDE IN YOUR IDEAL HEALING ENVIRONMENT?

_____
_____
_____
_____

HOW CAN YOU CREATE A PHYSICAL SPACE THAT SUPPORTS YOUR WELL-BEING AND HEALING JOURNEY?

_____
_____
_____
_____

I hold the
INTENTION

HOW DO YOU ENVISION THIS ENERGY MANIFESTING IN YOUR SACRED HEALING SPACE?

_____
_____
_____
_____
_____
_____
_____
_____

WHAT ELEMENTS CAN ENHANCE THE HEALING ATMOSPHERE?

_____
_____
_____
_____
_____
_____

HOW CAN GRATITUDE BECOME A PART OF YOUR DAILY PRACTICE?

_____
_____
_____
_____
_____
_____

WEEKLY PROGRESS / NOTABLE EXPERIENCES

Akahanama

Freedom to Choose, Freedom to Release,
Freedom to Be the Love that You Are

Step into bravery and pursue what you truly desire, as you explore your genuine self. The universe is on your side, so trust yourself and take a chance. This is your life to live authentically and find happiness. You are a unique expression of Love and it's your birthright to be who you're meant to be.

REFLECT ON DESIRES WITHIN YOU THAT YOU MAY HAVE BEEN HESITANT TO PURSUE. WHAT ARE ASPECTS OF YOURSELF THAT YOU GENUINELY WANT TO EXPLORE OR EMBRACE?

_____
_____
_____
_____

WHAT BRAVE STEPS CAN YOU TAKE TO ALIGN YOUR ACTIONS WITH YOUR GENUINE SELF?

_____
_____
_____
_____

My Authentic Self

HOW CAN YOU STRENGTHEN YOUR CONNECTION TO YOUR INNER WISDOM AND TRUST IN THE GUIDANCE IT PROVIDES?

WHAT CHANGES ALIGN WITH YOUR AUTHENTIC EXPRESSION OF SELF?

IN WHAT WAYS CAN YOU HONOR AND EMBODY THIS TRUTH IN YOUR DAILY LIFE?

WEEKLY PROGRESS / NOTABLE EXPERIENCES

Yah'tkh asks you to take a moment to slow down. This Code helps you focus your energy inward as you center yourself, and it can guide you as you expand your energy outward, to infinity.

TAKE A MOMENT TO REFLECT ON YOUR CURRENT PACE OF LIFE. DO YOU FIND YOURSELF RUSHING THROUGH TASKS AND ACTIVITIES?

_____
_____
_____
_____

PRACTICE CENTERING YOURSELF WITH AN INWARD FOCUS. WHAT ACTIVITIES OR TECHNIQUES HELP YOU TURN YOUR ENERGY INWARD AND FIND A SENSE OF INNER CALM?

_____
_____
_____
_____

my centering TECHNIQUES

HOW CAN YOU INTEGRATE MORE MOMENTS OF INWARD FOCUS INTO YOUR DAILY ROUTINE?

WHAT DOES IT MEAN TO YOU TO EXTEND YOUR ENERGY BEYOND YOUR IMMEDIATE SURROUNDINGS?

ARE THERE AREAS WHERE YOU COULD BENEFIT FROM MORE BALANCE BETWEEN INNER AND OUTER ENERGY?

HOW DOES THIS RESONATE WITH YOUR INNER AND OUTER PEACE?

WEEKLY PROGRESS / NOTABLE EXPERIENCES

Rugth

Being Centered and Grounded,
Gently Maintaining Respectful Boundaries

Rugth symbolizes potent boundary energies, usable in personal and professional spaces. It helps to find the root of dis-ease, re-establish personal power and create healthy boundaries. It's beneficial during shadow work, shifting our perspective towards a life full of love, respect and kindness.

REFLECT ON THE CONCEPT OF BOUNDARY ENERGIES IN YOUR LIFE. WHERE DO YOU FEEL THE NEED FOR STRONGER BOUNDARIES?

_____
_____
_____
_____

CONSIDER AREAS OF YOUR LIFE WHERE YOU MAY BE EXPERIENCING DIS-EASE. WHAT STEPS CAN YOU TAKE TO UNDERSTAND AND HEAL THE UNDERLYING ISSUES?

_____
_____
_____
_____

I AFFIRM

WHAT PRACTICES OR ACTIONS CAN YOU ENGAGE IN TO RECLAIM AND STRENGTHEN YOUR PERSONAL POWER?

HOW CAN YOU NAVIGATE AND INTEGRATE ASPECTS OF YOURSELF THAT MAY BE IN THE SHADOW?

WHAT BOUNDARIES ARE ESSENTIAL FOR CREATING A POSITIVE AND BALANCED LIFE?

HOW CAN YOU FOSTER A MINDSET THAT ALIGNS WITH EXPERIENCING LIFE FULL OF LOVE, RESPECT, AND KINDNESS?

WEEKLY PROGRESS / NOTABLE EXPERIENCES

Scryb'th

Warming the Heart, Supporting a Healthy Path, Expanding Self

Scryb'th aids your healing and unlocks your potential, bringing safety and sanctuary as your Heart expands. You may find your intuition improving, so don't be afraid to listen to that soft inner voice. Ask, "What's in my highest good?" and listen for the mysterious answers.

REFLECT ON YOUR CURRENT HEALING JOURNEY. IN WHAT AREAS OF YOUR LIFE DO YOU SEEK HEALING?

_____
_____
_____
_____

WHAT EMOTIONS OR THOUGHTS ARISE AS YOU ENVISION SAFETY AND SANCTUARY?

_____
_____
_____
_____

I Shine BRIGHTLY

WHAT CHANGES OR ACTIONS MIGHT INSPIRE YOU TO EMBRACE THE FREEDOM AND TRANSFORMATIVE ENERGY?

HOW CAN YOU CREATE SPACE IN YOUR LIFE TO REGULARLY LISTEN FOR GUIDANCE FROM YOUR HEART?

HOW OPEN ARE YOU TO RECEIVING GUIDANCE FROM UNEXPECTED SOURCES?

WEEKLY PROGRESS / NOTABLE EXPERIENCES

Ahagma

Integrating, Taking the Next Step, Releasing Resistance, Making Progres

Ahagma integrates lessons, healing, and experiences, empowering and inspiring us. Be brave, take the next step, and release resistance manifested as anger, fear, sadness, or confusion.

TAKE A MOMENT TO REFLECT ON THE LESSONS AND HEALINGS YOU'VE EXPERIENCED. HOW HAVE THESE SHAPED YOUR JOURNEY?

_____
_____
_____
_____

IDENTIFY AN AREA OF YOUR LIFE WHERE YOU FEEL THE CALL TO TAKE THE NEXT STEP. WHAT SPECIFIC ACTIONS CAN YOU TAKE TO ALIGN WITH IT?

_____
_____
_____
_____

REFLECT ON ANY RESISTANCE YOU MAY BE EXPERIENCING, IS IT IN THE FORM OF ANGER, FEAR, SADNESS, OR CONFUSION? WHAT STEPS CAN YOU TAKE TO CULTIVATE A MINDSET OF OPENNESS AND ACCEPTANCE?

WHAT UNDERLYING EMOTIONS OR BELIEFS CONTRIBUTE TO THIS RESISTANCE?

- [ ] _____
- [ ] _____
- [ ] _____
- [ ] _____
- [ ] _____
- [ ] _____
- [ ] _____

HOW CAN ENSURE THAT YOU ARE MOVING FORWARD IN ALIGNMENT?

- [ ] _____
- [ ] _____
- [ ] _____
- [ ] _____
- [ ] _____
- [ ] _____

"by honoring our past but not living there, we can heal.."
~LAARA

WEEKLY PROGRESS / NOTABLE EXPERIENCES

Kh'mak

Time, Presence, Flow, Freedom, Breath

Kh'mak's message is clear: slow down and notice something in your perception. It's about time, freedom, and flow, where flow brings freedom without resistance. Take a deep breath, focus on the present moment, and embrace yourself in all your perfection.

TAKE A MOMENT TO REFLECT ON YOUR CURRENT PERCEPTION OF LIFE. ARE THERE ASPECTS OR DETAILS THAT YOU MIGHT BE OVERLOOKING?

_____
_____
_____
_____
_____

CONSIDER MOMENTS IN YOUR LIFE WHEN YOU HAVE FELT IN FLOW— COMPLETELY PRESENT AND FREE. WHAT ACTIVITIES OR CIRCUMSTANCES CONTRIBUTE TO THIS SENSE OF FLOW FOR YOU?

_____
_____
_____
_____
_____

I am in THE PRESENT

HOW CAN YOU CULTIVATE MINDFULNESS AND AWARENESS IN YOUR DAILY ACTIVITIES?

HOW CAN YOU RELEASE RESISTANCE AND EMBRACE THE UNFOLDING OF LIFE AROUND YOU?

WHAT STEPS CAN YOU TAKE TO SURRENDER TO THE PRESENT MOMENT?

WEEKLY PROGRESS / NOTABLE EXPERIENCES

Turla

Stillpoint

Turla reveals that emotional reactions to challenges create chaotic energy. Reacting more makes it worse, as we get caught in an escalating loop of chaos. Our ability to find peace can be a challenge, but we all have a beautiful stillpoint within us to access. Practicing non-reactivity restores harmony within and makes us less reactive.

REFLECT ON RECENT CHALLENGES IN YOUR LIFE THAT TRIGGERED EMOTIONAL REACTIONS. IN WHAT WAYS DID THE VOLATILITY OF YOUR EMOTIONS AFFECT YOUR OVERALL SENSE OF WELL-BEING?

___

___

___

___

CONSIDER INSTANCES WHERE YOUR REACTIONS ESCALATED INTO A LOOP OF CHAOS. HOW CAN RECOGNIZING THESE PATTERNS BE A STEP TOWARD BREAKING THE CYCLE?

___

___

___

___

my harmonious SELF

HOW CAN YOU ACKNOWLEDGE AND CONNECT WITH YOUR INNER HOME?

IN WHAT AREAS OF YOUR LIFE DO YOU FIND IT CHALLENGING TO PRACTICE NON-REACTIVITY?

HOW CAN CREATING A PRACTICE CONTRIBUTE TO RESTORING HARMONY IN YOUR ENERGY AND RESPONSES?

WEEKLY PROGRESS / NOTABLE EXPERIENCES

Tsuhami

Butterfly Wings:
Spread Your Wings and Fly,
Release Resistance, Trust

Tsuhami says you've done good work and awakened your true power. Let go, free yourself, and live your highest purpose. Transform yourself to become who you're meant to be. Find the right flowers in the right gardens to nourish and support you. Grow, flourish, and step into a miraculous life.

LOOK BACK ON YOUR JOURNEY OF INNER TRANSFORMATION. WHAT ASPECTS OF YOURSELF HAVE YOU WORKED ON, AND HOW HAVE YOU AWAKENED YOUR TRUE POWER?

_____
_____
_____
_____

WHAT ACHIEVEMENTS, BIG OR SMALL, MAKE YOU PROUD OF THE WORK YOU'VE DONE WITHIN YOURSELF?

_____
_____
_____
_____

I release RESISTANCE

WHAT ATTACHMENTS, BELIEFS, OR HABITS ARE NO LONGER SERVING YOUR HIGHEST PURPOSE?

HOW CAN RELEASING THESE ELEMENTS FREE YOU TO STEP INTO THE NEXT PHASE OF YOUR JOURNEY?

HOW CAN YOU ALIGN YOUR ACTIONS TO YOUR HIGHEST PURPOSE?

WHAT ENVIRONMENTS, RELATIONSHIPS, OR ACTIVITIES NURTURE YOUR GROWTH AND FLOURISHING?

WEEKLY PROGRESS / NOTABLE EXPERIENCES

Turmar

Unity

Turmar vibrates with unity in Self and helps establish a connection with your higher self. To connect, we must dismantle our egos and align with the unifying forces of Heart expansion. Engaging with Turmar accesses inner knowing and Self-Love, moving away from seeking answers outside ourselves, and into the strength of our empowered Self.

REFLECT ON YOUR UNDERSTANDING OF UNITY WITHIN YOURSELF. HOW DO YOU CURRENTLY EXPERIENCE THIS CONCEPT?

_____
_____
_____
_____

CONSIDER YOUR RELATIONSHIP WITH YOUR HIGHER SELF. HOW DO YOU CURRENTLY COMMUNICATE WITH THIS ASPECT OF YOURSELF?

_____
_____
_____
_____

I Shine BRIGHTLY

WHAT ASPECTS OF THE EGO MIGHT BE HINDERING YOUR CONNECTION TO UNITY AND HIGHER SELF?

HOW CAN YOU DISMANTLE THE EGO FOR A HARMONIOUS, ALIGNED EXISTENCE?

HOW CAN I EMBRACE MORE SELF-LOVE?

WEEKLY PROGRESS / NOTABLE EXPERIENCES

Teglih

Healing the Physical Plane
(Mother Earth, Her Plants, and the Physical Body)

Teglih symbolizes healing beyond time and space, usable on anyone or anything by bringing them to mind. It's also a symbol of blessing; speaking its name aloud is powerful and can be used in prayer.

CONSIDER INSTANCES IN YOUR LIFE WHERE HEALING ENERGIES HAVE PLAYED A ROLE. HOW HAVE YOU EXPERIENCED HEALING, WHETHER PERSONALLY OR WITNESSED IN OTHERS?

_____
_____
_____
_____

CONSIDER INSTANCES IN YOUR LIFE WHERE HEALING ENERGIES HAVE PLAYED A ROLE. HOW HAVE YOU EXPERIENCED HEALING, WHETHER PERSONALLY OR WITNESSED IN OTHERS?

_____
_____
_____
_____

CONTEMPLATE THE PROCESS OF BRINGING RECIPIENTS INTO YOUR CONSCIOUS MIND FOR HEALING WITH TEGLIH. HOW CAN YOU INTENTIONALLY FOCUS ON INDIVIDUALS OR SITUATIONS THAT COULD BENEFIT FROM HEALING ENERGY?

WHAT PRACTICES CAN YOU ESTABLISH TO BRING RECIPIENTS INTO YOUR CONSCIOUS AWARENESS?

- [ ] _____
- [ ] _____
- [ ] _____
- [ ] _____
- [ ] _____
- [ ] _____
- [ ] _____

HOW MIGHT YOU DEEPEN YOUR CONNECTION WITH THE DIVINE OR THE SOURCE OF HEALING?

- [ ] _____
- [ ] _____
- [ ] _____
- [ ] _____
- [ ] _____
- [ ] _____
- [ ] _____

"We are all interconnected. Every action we take should come from the Heart."

~LAARA

WEEKLY PROGRESS / NOTABLE EXPERIENCES

Kahlsi symbolizes interconnectedness and the importance of our thoughts, feelings, and actions. It reminds us to act from the Heart with Love, creativity, clarity, and compassion, inspiring and uplifting others along the way.

REFLECT ON THE CONCEPT OF INTERCONNECTEDNESS. HOW DOES THIS IDEA RESONATE WITH YOUR UNDERSTANDING OF THE WORLD AND YOUR PLACE IN IT?

EXPLORE THE IMPORTANCE OF LIVING FROM THE HEART. HOW CAN YOU ENSURE THAT YOUR THOUGHTS AND ACTIONS COME FROM A PLACE OF GENUINE COMPASSION AND LOVE?

I am CONNECTED

HOW DO YOUR THOUGHTS, WORDS, AND ACTIONS INSPIRE AND UPLIFT THOSE AROUND YOU?

HOW CAN YOU INFUSE MORE CREATIVITY AND CLARITY INTO YOUR DAILY ACTIVITIES?

HOW CAN YOU CAN YOU BRING A COMPASSIONATE PERSPECTIVE TO ENHANCE YOUR ENGAGEMENT WITH LIFE?

WEEKLY PROGRESS / NOTABLE EXPERIENCES

Hydahama holds an energy free from confusion, and resides in a place of Love where there is only pure truth. It assists us in letting go of the challenges we face, by helping us adopt multiple perspectives. This Code excels at guiding us through difficult situations by suggesting other options and responses which allow for healing, growth and advancement.

REFLECT ON PAST OBSTACLES YOU'VE ENCOUNTERED. HOW DID YOU APPROACH THEM EMOTIONALLY?

_____
_____
_____
_____

EXPLORE MOMENTS IN YOUR LIFE WHEN YOU FELT CLOSED OFF DUE TO FEAR OR HATE. HOW DID THESE EMOTIONS IMPACT YOUR ABILITY TO NAVIGATE THOSE SITUATIONS?

_____
_____
_____
_____

My Harmonious Self

HOW CAN ADOPTING MULTIPLE PERSPECTIVES ENHANCE YOUR DECISION-MAKING AND APPROACH TO CHALLENGES?

_____
_____
_____
_____
_____
_____
_____
_____
_____
_____

HOW DO YOU NAVIGATE EXPRESSING YOUR TRUTH WHILE REMAINING COMPASSIONATE?

_____
_____
_____
_____
_____
_____
_____

WHAT STEPS CAN YOU TAKE TO OPEN UP TO GREATER PERSONAL GROWTH, HEALING, AND EXPANSION IN YOUR LIFE?

_____
_____
_____
_____
_____
_____
_____

WEEKLY PROGRESS / NOTABLE EXPERIENCES

Bahan

Forgiveness

Bahan reminds us that forgiveness is essential for a fulfilling life. This Code helps to heal fragmented energy and smooth out difficulties in relationships. By tapping into our integrity and drawing our Love forward, we can cut through the confusion and bring clarity to difficult situations.

REFLECT ON MOMENTS WHEN YOU MAY HAVE FELT LIKE YOU LEFT YOUR HEART BEHIND IN THE MIDST OF CONFUSION. WHAT SITUATIONS OR RELATIONSHIPS LED TO THIS FEELING? HOW DID IT IMPACT YOUR WELL-BEING AND INTERACTIONS?

___

___

___

___

EXPLORE YOUR UNDERSTANDING OF FORGIVENESS. IN WHAT WAYS DOES FORGIVENESS CONTRIBUTE TO FLOURISHING IN A WORLD FILLED WITH CHALLENGES?

___

___

___

___

I choose FORGIVENESS

WHAT ASPECTS OF FORGIVENESS AND LOVE CAN YOU TAP INTO TO SMOOTH OUT DIFFICULTIES?

HOW CAN ALIGNING WITH YOUR INTEGRITY CONTRIBUTE TO CLARITY AND RESOLUTION?

WHAT DOES INTEGRITY MEAN TO YOU?

WHAT PRACTICES OR MINDSET SHIFTS CAN ASSIST YOU IN BRINGING WARMTH AND LOVE TO COLD-HEARTED SITUATIONS?

WEEKLY PROGRESS / NOTABLE EXPERIENCES

Halahma

Finding Inner Fire, Strength, and Clarity

Halahma helps us overcome addictive or abusive tendencies by bringing forth our inner strength and clarity. With its healing fire, we can take back our power and find the strength to let go of negative habits and patterns.

REFLECT ON YOUR OWN TENDENCIES, WHETHER THEY ARE RELATED TO EMOTIONS, OR HABITUAL. WHAT PATTERNS DO YOU NOTICE? HOW DO THESE TENDENCIES IMPACT YOUR WELL-BEING AND DAILY LIFE?

_____
_____
_____
_____
_____

REFLECT ON MOMENTS IN YOUR LIFE WHEN YOU FELT A DEEP SENSE OF INNER STRENGTH. WHAT SOURCES OF STRENGTH WERE PRESENT IN THOSE MOMENTS?

_____
_____
_____
_____
_____

I am STRONG

HOW CAN YOU INVITE HALAHMA'S GUIDANCE INTO YOUR LIFE TO ADDRESS ADDICTIVE TENDENCIES?

HOW CAN YOU DRAW UPON STRENGTH TO NAVIGATE CHALLENGES RELATED TO ADDICTIVE OR ABUSIVE TENDENCIES?

HOW CAN YOU CONNECT WITH AND NOURISH THE HEALING FIRE WITHIN YOURSELF?

HOW CAN THIS INTERNAL FIRE CONTRIBUTE TO YOUR JOURNEY OF HEALING AND TRANSFORMATION?

WEEKLY PROGRESS / NOTABLE EXPERIENCES

Khalagma

Releasing Mis-Qualified Energies, Removing Obstacles

Khalagma can help us release limiting beliefs and energies that prevent us from achieving our goals. By letting go of negative thoughts and feelings, we can live more in alignment with our purpose. You can use Khalagma on its own or with your favourite shadow work/belief work practices for further growth and healing.

REFLECT ON BELIEFS THAT MAY BE STANDING IN THE WAY OF WHAT YOU WISH TO HAVE IN LIFE. HOW DO THESE BELIEFS INFLUENCE YOUR ACTIONS AND DECISIONS?

_____
_____
_____
_____
_____

WHERE DO YOU FEEL RESISTANCE OR STAGNATION? HOW MIGHT THESE ENERGETIC BLOCKAGES BE HINDERING YOUR PROGRESS TOWARD YOUR GOALS AND HIGHEST PURPOSE?

_____
_____
_____
_____
_____

I Release
NEGATIVITY

HOW CAN YOU ACTIVELY SEEK KHALAGMA'S GUIDANCE IN RELEASING ENERGIES THAT NO LONGER SERVE YOU?

HOW CAN YOU APPROACH SHADOW WORK WITH A SENSE OF COMPASSION AND SELF-DISCOVERY?

HOW CAN YOU ACTIVELY CULTIVATE BELIEFS AND ENERGIES THAT SUPPORT YOUR JOURNEY TOWARD YOUR HIGHEST PURPOSE?

ADD A LITTLE BIT OF BODY TEXT

Hoitma

Cleansing Breath, Clearing Lungs

Hoitma reminds us of the power of breath to revitalize our entire being. The movement of oxygen, the breath of life, energizes every cell in our body, and every ion in our energy field. This Code helps us bring freedom to the parts of our being that feels restricted, like expanding our lungs to take a full, deep, and invigorating breath.

REFLECT ON YOUR AWARENESS OF THE POWER OF BREATH IN REVITALIZING THE BODY. IN WHAT WAYS HAVE YOU EXPERIENCED THE IMPACT OF BREATH ON YOUR PHYSICAL AND MENTAL STATE?

_____
_____
_____
_____

REFLECT ON YOUR CURRENT BREATHING PATTERNS. DO YOU NOTICE ANY RESTRICTIONS OR SHALLOW BREATHING? HOW MIGHT AN INCREASED AWARENESS OF YOUR BREATH LEAD TO POSITIVE CHANGES IN YOUR OVERALL WELL-BEING?

_____
_____
_____
_____

CONSIDER THE MESSAGE THAT THERE MAY BE SOMETHING OR SOMEONE INHIBITING YOUR SENSE OF FREEDOM. WHAT ASPECTS OF YOUR LIFE OR RELATIONSHIPS MIGHT BE CONTRIBUTING TO THIS INHIBITION?

HOW CAN YOU ADDRESS OR RELEASE THESE INHIBITIONS TO FOSTER A GREATER SENSE OF FREEDOM?

- [ ] _____
- [ ] _____
- [ ] _____
- [ ] _____
- [ ] _____
- [ ] _____
- [ ] _____

WHAT SPECIFIC ACTIONS CAN YOU TAKE TO CREATE AN ENVIRONMENT THAT NURTURES YOUR SENSE OF FREEDOM?

- [ ] _____
- [ ] _____
- [ ] _____
- [ ] _____
- [ ] _____
- [ ] _____
- [ ] _____

"Breathe balance into your Self..."
~LAARA

WEEKLY PROGRESS / NOTABLE EXPERIENCES

Pain is our body's way of communicating something needs attention. Sometimes it's useful to become conscious of the story behind the pain; other times it's not. This Code's energy assists in any needed insight to come to light, and helps to release your physical discomfort.

CONTEMPLATE THE IDEA THAT PAIN IS THE BODY'S WAY OF COMMUNICATING A PROBLEM. HOW DO YOU CURRENTLY PERCEIVE THE PURPOSE OF PAIN IN YOUR LIFE?

_____
_____
_____
_____

IN WHAT SITUATIONS HAVE YOU FOUND IT USEFUL TO BECOME CONSCIOUS OF THE STORY BEHIND THE PAIN? HOW DID THIS EXPLORATION CONTRIBUTE TO YOUR UNDERSTANDING OF THE PAIN?

_____
_____
_____
_____

I RELEASE

WHAT SPECIFIC ACTIONS OR PRACTICES CAN YOU INCORPORATE INTO YOUR ROUTINE TO FACILITATE THIS RELEASE?

IN WHAT WAYS MIGHT YOU BE OPEN TO RECEIVING INSIGHTS ABOUT YOUR PHYSICAL DISCOMFORT?

HOW MIGHT THIS APPROACH ALIGN WITH YOUR OVERALL WELL-BEING?

WEEKLY PROGRESS / NOTABLE EXPERIENCES

Even as we face challenges, there is beauty and sweetness to be found... we just need to remember to look! Each petal offers a unique perspective on life. Observe their directions, planes and possibilities to view your circumstances softly from multiple angles. Discover beauty and peace in everything, and seek the vast wisdom and knowledge of your infinite being.

BEGIN BY TRACING THE LINES OF THE SYMBOL WITH YOUR EYES OR FINGERS. WHAT SENSATIONS OR THOUGHTS ARISE AS YOU FOLLOW THE LINES?

_____
_____
_____
_____

CONSIDER EACH PETAL OF THE SYMBOL AS OFFERING A DIFFERENT PERSPECTIVE ON YOUR LIFE AND CIRCUMSTANCES. HOW MIGHT VIEWING YOUR CHALLENGES OR SITUATIONS FROM MULTIPLE ANGLES ENRICH YOUR UNDERSTANDING?

_____
_____
_____
_____

I find PEACE

HOW MIGHT EMBRACING THE IDEA OF MULTIPLE POSSIBILITIES INFLUENCE YOUR DECISION-MAKING AND OUTLOOK?

_____
_____
_____
_____
_____
_____
_____
_____
_____
_____

HOW DOES ADOPTING A SOFTER, MORE OPEN MINDSET IMPACT YOUR PERCEPTION OF CHALLENGES?

_____
_____
_____
_____
_____
_____

ARE THERE SPECIFIC PRACTICES, HABITS, OR MINDSET SHIFTS THAT COULD CONTRIBUTE TO A GREATER SENSE OF WELL-BEING?

_____
_____
_____
_____
_____
_____
_____

WEEKLY PROGRESS / NOTABLE EXPERIENCES

Pahma

Love of the Highest Order

Love is all around you... everywhere, and within reach at all times. Pahma embodies pure Love, a powerful force that can heal the energetic imbalances causing confusion, pain and suffering. It holds the frequency to help us reconnect with Love and is a beacon of hope for those seeking peace. Panma is an expression of Love of the Highest Order.

REFLECT ON YOUR CURRENT UNDERSTANDING OF LOVE. HOW DO YOU DEFINE LOVE IN YOUR LIFE? IN WHAT WAYS MIGHT YOUR PERCEPTION OF LOVE HAVE EVOLVED OR BEEN INFLUENCED BY PAST EXPERIENCES?

_____
_____
_____
_____
_____

CONSIDER THE IDEA THAT LOVE HEALS ENERGETIC DISTURBANCES WITHIN AND AROUND YOU. WHAT ENERGETIC DISTURBANCES OR CHALLENGES DO YOU CURRENTLY FACE?

_____
_____
_____
_____
_____

I choose LOVE

HOW MIGHT YOU CONNECT WITH AND CULTIVATE A SENSE OF PURE LOVE IN YOUR DAILY LIFE?

WHAT MEMORIES OR EXPERIENCES EVOKE A DEEP SENSE OF LOVE FOR YOU?

_____
_____
_____
_____
_____

WHAT DO YOU LOVE MOST IN YOUR LIFE?

_____
_____
_____
_____
_____

HOW CAN YOU ACTIVELY ENGAGE IN THE REMEMBRANCE OF LOVE TO ENHANCE YOUR OVERALL WELL-BEING?

_____
_____
_____
_____
_____

WEEKLY PROGRESS / NOTABLE EXPERIENCES

Lahma

Non-Attachment, Letting Go, Freedom

Attachments can be to people, places, things, or to emotions, patterns, and behaviors. Letting go of our attachments is an art that requires practice. Lahma teaches non-attachment as a skill to navigate life's challenges. With practice, letting go becomes easier, and you can steer through life's seas more effortlessly.

REFLECT ON THE VARIOUS ASPECTS OF YOUR LIFE TO WHICH YOU FEEL ATTACHED. WHAT ATTACHMENTS STAND OUT TO YOU? HOW DO THESE ATTACHMENTS INFLUENCE YOUR DAILY LIFE AND WELL-BEING?

_____
_____
_____
_____

EXPLORE THE ART OF LETTING GO. WHAT DOES LETTING GO MEAN TO YOU, AND HOW HAVE YOU PRACTICED IT IN THE PAST?

_____
_____
_____
_____

I let go of ATTACHMENTS

ARE THERE SPECIFIC SITUATIONS WHERE LETTING GO HAS BEEN CHALLENGING OR LIBERATING?

ARE THERE SPECIFIC AREAS WHERE YOU SEEK GUIDANCE IN CULTIVATING NON-ATTACHMENT?

IN WHAT WAYS MIGHT NON-ATTACHMENT SERVE AS A COMPASS OR GUIDE?

HOW MIGHT EMBRACING NON-ATTACHMENT POSITIVELY IMPACT YOUR OVERALL WELL-BEING?

WEEKLY PROGRESS / NOTABLE EXPERIENCES

Henama

Healing Sexual Abuse and Trauma

Henama symbolizes healing through playfulness and whimsy while embodying integrity, strength, and authority. It encourages disregarding opinions that don't align with Love. Embracing this energy creates a powerful space where Love is the foundation for events, creations, and relationships to flourish.

REFLECT ON THE CONCEPT OF PLAY AND WHIMSY AS HEALING ENERGIES. IN WHAT WAYS CAN EMBRACING A SENSE OF WHIMSY CONTRIBUTE TO YOUR OVERALL WELL-BEING?

CONTEMPLATE THE IDEA THAT HENAMA EMBODIES BOTH PLAYFULNESS AND INTEGRITY. HOW DO YOU PERCEIVE THE RELATIONSHIP BETWEEN THESE QUALITIES?

I Release
TRAUMA

HOW DO YOU CURRENTLY NAVIGATE DIFFERING OPINIONS?

ARE THERE AREAS WHERE YOU CAN INTENTIONALLY INFUSE MORE PLAY AND INTEGRITY?

WHAT SPECIFIC ACTIONS CAN YOU TAKE TO EMBODY PLAY, WHIMSY, AND INTEGRITY IN YOUR DAILY INTERACTIONS?

WEEKLY PROGRESS / NOTABLE EXPERIENCES

Aman'ka encourages us to take a closer look at our lives, to observe the ways in which we are both in and out of alignment with our Heart. Check if events and energies align with Heart's happiness. Surrender, trust, and embrace any necessary changes, knowing your Heart can lead you to perfect alignments.

BEGIN BY REFLECTING ON THE CURRENT EVENTS, DYNAMICS, OR ENERGIES IN YOUR LIFE. HOW DO THESE ELEMENTS ALIGN WITH YOUR SENSE OF WELL-BEING AND HAPPINESS?

_____
_____
_____
_____
_____

WHAT BRINGS JOY AND FULFILLMENT TO YOUR HEART? IN WHAT AREAS OF YOUR LIFE DO YOU FEEL A SENSE OF ALIGNMENT WITH YOUR TRUE DESIRES AND VALUES?

_____
_____
_____
_____
_____

TAKE TIME TO EXPLORE YOUR INNER FEELINGS AND RESPONSES. ARE THERE ASPECTS OF YOUR LIFE THAT MAY REQUIRE ADJUSTMENT OR REALIGNMENT WITH YOUR HEART'S DESIRES?

IN WHAT WAYS CAN YOU CULTIVATE A DEEPER SENSE OF TRUST IN YOUR JOURNEY?

- [ ]
- [ ]
- [ ]
- [ ]
- [ ]
- [ ]
- [ ]

HOW CAN UNEXPECTED BEAUTY GUIDE YOU IN NAVIGATING CURRENT CHALLENGES?

- [ ]
- [ ]
- [ ]
- [ ]
- [ ]
- [ ]
- [ ]

"Walk gently. Your participation on earth is celebrated..."

~LAARA

WEEKLY PROGRESS / NOTABLE EXPERIENCES

Jamaka reminds you to take things slowly, relax, and release burdens. Trust that everything unfolds perfectly, and let go of life's pressures. Use this symbol to find your center and feel grounded, centered, and in the flow. There's no need for stress.

REFLECT ON THE CURRENT ENERGIES IN YOUR LIFE THAT MAY FEEL BURDENSOME. WHAT PRESSURES OR STRESSORS ARE YOU EXPERIENCING? HOW DO THESE ENERGIES IMPACT YOUR OVERALL WELL-BEING AND SENSE OF PEACE?

_____
_____
_____
_____

HOW MIGHT BREAKING DOWN TASKS OR CHALLENGES INTO SMALLER STEPS ALLEVIATE THE SENSE OF BURDEN? IN WHAT AREAS OF YOUR LIFE CAN YOU APPLY THE PRINCIPLE OF TAKING THINGS ONE STEP AT A TIME?

_____
_____
_____
_____

I am CENTERED

WHAT PRACTICES OR TECHNIQUES DO YOU CURRENTLY USE TO RELAX AND RELEASE TENSION?

HOW MIGHT TRUSTING IN PERFECT OUTCOMES ALLEVIATE UNNECESSARY WORRY OR STRESS?

HOW CAN YOU CULTIVATE A SENSE OF GROUNDEDNESS, CENTERING, AND BEING 'IN THE FLOW' IN YOUR DAILY LIFE?

WEEKLY PROGRESS / NOTABLE EXPERIENCES

Akuna

Trusting Your Experience, Belonging

Trust the eternal quantum field and find oneness within. Akuna reminds you that you belong everywhere and encourages you to express love beyond measure by connecting with all things through your heart's infinite wisdom. Rise above the ego mind and trust in the equality of all beings.

> HOW DO YOU CURRENTLY PERCEIVE TRUST IN THE BROADER CONTEXT OF LIFE AND EXISTENCE? IN WHAT WAYS CAN THE CONCEPT OF THE QUANTUM FIELD INFLUENCE YOUR UNDERSTANDING OF TRUST?

_____
_____
_____
_____

> ARE THERE AREAS IN YOUR LIFE WHERE YOU FEEL A SENSE OF BELONGING, OR ARE THERE ASPECTS WHERE YOU CAN CONSCIOUSLY CULTIVATE A STRONGER CONNECTION?

_____
_____
_____
_____

I trust MYSELF

WHAT PRACTICES OR MOMENTS ALLOW YOU TO STEP ABOVE THE EGO MIND AND EXPRESS LOVE AND CONNECTIVITY FROM THE HEART?

HOW MIGHT TRUSTING IN ONENESS IMPACT YOUR PERSPECTIVE ON CHALLENGES AND RELATIONSHIPS?

HOW CAN YOU BRAVELY EXPRESS LOVE IN YOUR INTERACTIONS AND RELATIONSHIPS?

WEEKLY PROGRESS / NOTABLE EXPERIENCES

Yunami

Remember, Reflect, Gain Clarity, Make Connections

Embrace a higher purpose and find clarity in connections. Yunami calls you to expand your spiritual practice or choose one that suits you. This symbol represents making connections and identifies imbalanced relationships that no longer serve you. Gratefully let go of those relationships and honor all involved.

HOW MIGHT EMBRACING A HIGHER PURPOSE CONTRIBUTE TO A SENSE OF FULFILLMENT AND MEANING IN YOUR LIFE?

_____
_____
_____
_____

IN WHAT AREAS OF YOUR LIFE DO YOU SEEK GREATER CLARITY? HOW CAN YOU ACTIVELY CULTIVATE CONNECTIONS THAT ALIGN WITH YOUR HIGHER PURPOSE?

_____
_____
_____
_____

I am CONNECTED

WHAT SPIRITUAL PRACTICES RESONATE WITH YOU, AND HOW DO THEY CONTRIBUTE TO YOUR WELL-BEING?

HOW CAN YOU EXPRESS GRATITUDE FOR THE LESSONS AND EXPERIENCES SHARED?

IN WHAT WAYS CAN YOU HONOR THE GROWTH THAT HAS OCCURRED?

WHAT QUALITIES AND CONNECTIONS SUPPORT YOUR JOURNEY TOWARD A HIGHER PURPOSE?

WEEKLY PROGRESS / NOTABLE EXPERIENCES

Humbelah

Heart Full of Gratitude

Humbelah symbolizes and radiates gratitude in every line and curve. It can assist in rediscovering gratitude or amplifying it if you already have a connection to it. Being thankful is a key part of conscious manifestation, and naturally radiates from our heart, making it an essential component of a fulfilling life.

HOW OFTEN DO YOU CONSCIOUSLY EXPERIENCE GRATITUDE IN YOUR DAILY LIFE?

_____
_____
_____
_____

IN WHAT SITUATIONS OR ASPECTS OF YOUR LIFE DO YOU FIND IT EASY OR CHALLENGING TO FEEL GRATITUDE?

_____
_____
_____
_____

My heart is in GRATITUDE

HOW CAN YOU DEEPEN YOUR EXISTING SENSE OF GRATITUDE?

HOW DOES THE CONCEPT OF ABUNDANCE RELATE TO GRATITUDE IN YOUR LIFE?

IN WHAT WAYS CAN YOU INCORPORATE GRATITUDE INTO YOUR MANIFESTATION PRACTICES?

WHAT CAN HELP YOU CULTIVATE A HEART-CENTERED APPROACH TO GRATITUDE?

WEEKLY PROGRESS / NOTABLE EXPERIENCES

Delight

Seeing Clearly, No Confusion: Remembering Who We Are

Delight holds a powerful message, trust that your path is unfolding perfectly. Embrace your power as a being of love and beauty. Use Delight during a full or new moon to seek truth within and around you. Affirm love and use it daily or during a moon ceremony.

TAKE A MOMENT TO REFLECT ON YOUR CURRENT LIFE PATH. WHAT ASPECTS OF YOUR JOURNEY BRING YOU DELIGHT AND JOY?

_____
_____
_____
_____
_____

HOW DO YOU DEFINE YOUR PERSONAL POWER? IN WHAT WAYS CAN YOU CONSCIOUSLY TAP INTO AND EXPRESS THE LOVE AND BEAUTY WITHIN YOURSELF?

_____
_____
_____
_____
_____

I see CLEARLY

WHAT DOES INNER TRUTH MEAN TO YOU?

ARE THERE PRACTICES OR ACTIVITIES THAT HELP YOU CONNECT WITH YOUR INNER TRUTH?

HOW CAN YOU BECOME MORE AWARE OF THE LOVE THAT SURROUNDS YOU IN YOUR DAILY LIFE?

WEEKLY PROGRESS / NOTABLE EXPERIENCES

Kahalula

The Love Felt Between Twin Souls

Kahalula emphasizes the healing potential of the Twin relationship if both parties are willing to work on themselves. Healing oneself benefits others and all beings. Triggers may surface for healing and can be viewed positively with a greater perspective.

HOW DO YOU PERCEIVE THE CONCEPT OF A TWIN RELATIONSHIP IN YOUR LIFE? ARE THERE RELATIONSHIPS THAT RESONATE WITH THE IDEA OF DEEP HEALING?

_____
_____
_____
_____

IN WHAT WAYS HAVE YOU EXPERIENCED HEALING WITHIN YOURSELF THROUGH RELATIONSHIPS? HOW MIGHT YOUR HEALING JOURNEY POSITIVELY IMPACT OTHERS?

_____
_____
_____
_____

CAN YOU IDENTIFY ANY TRIGGERS IN YOUR CURRENT RELATIONSHIPS OR EXPERIENCES? HOW MIGHT REFRAMING THESE TRIGGERS AS OPPORTUNITIES FOR HEALING SHIFT YOUR PERSPECTIVE?

ARE THERE AREAS IN YOUR LIFE WHERE YOU FEEL READY TO ENGAGE IN DEEPER HEALING WORK?

- [ ]
- [ ]
- [ ]
- [ ]
- [ ]
- [ ]
- [ ]

HOW CAN THIS CONTRIBUTE TO THE WELL-BEING OF BOTH YOURSELF AND OTHERS?

- [ ]
- [ ]
- [ ]
- [ ]
- [ ]
- [ ]
- [ ]

"Walk gently. Your participation on earth is celebrated..."

~LAARA

WEEKLY PROGRESS / NOTABLE EXPERIENCES

Pahgyahma symbolizes healing, protection, life, uplifting emotions, and energy building. It integrates the healing properties of the Sun and Earth, connecting us to their energies with ease. Use it to deepen your connection to these energies.

REFLECT ON THE SYMBOLIC ENERGIES ASSOCIATED WITH PAHGYAHMA. HOW DO THESE ENERGIES RESONATE WITH YOUR CURRENT LIFE EXPERIENCES?

_____
_____
_____
_____
_____

HOW DO YOU CURRENTLY CONNECT WITH THE ENERGIES OF THE SUN AND EARTH IN YOUR DAILY LIFE? ARE THERE PRACTICES OR RITUALS YOU CAN INCORPORATE TO DEEPEN THIS CONNECTION AND INTEGRATION?

_____
_____
_____
_____
_____

I can
CONNECT

WHAT COME FORWARD WITH SUN ENERGY?	WHAT COMES FORWARD WITH EARTH ENERGY

WEEKLY PROGRESS / NOTABLE EXPERIENCES

Yahma transfers frequencies between objects and facilitates communication with angels, guides, and other Spirits of the Light. Enhance channeling abilities, strengthen gifts and talents, and anchor them in the physical body.

> REFLECT ON THE IDEA THAT YAHMA CAN BE USED TO TRANSFER FREQUENCIES FROM ONE OBJECT TO ANOTHER. ARE THERE SPECIFIC AREAS OF YOUR LIFE WHERE YOU FEEL THE NEED FOR A SHIFT OR ENHANCEMENT IN ENERGY?

_____
_____
_____
_____

> CONSIDER THE NOTION THAT YAHMA CAN ASSIST IN COMMUNICATING ACROSS DIMENSIONS WITH ANGELS, GUIDES, OR OTHER SPIRITS OF THE LIGHT. ARE THERE SPECIFIC SPIRITUAL BEINGS OR ENERGIES YOU WOULD LIKE TO CONNECT WITH THROUGH THIS SYMBOL?

_____
_____
_____
_____

I see
CLEARLY

HOW DO YOU CURRENTLY PERCEIVE YOUR CHANNELING CAPABILITIES?

WHAT ARE YOUR UNIQUE GIFTS AND ABILITIES?

ARE THERE PRACTICES OR RITUALS THAT CAN HELP YOU EMBODY AND EXPRESS THESE GIFTS MORE FULLY?

WEEKLY PROGRESS / NOTABLE EXPERIENCES

Call upon Light Beings for assistance. Envision and feel Spirit while gazing at the symbol. Ask simple questions to establish clear communication and emotional connection. Thank and bless the Spirit and Hennami for facilitating and protecting the sacred space.

REFLECT ON THE IDEA THAT EVERYONE HAS A GROUP OF LIGHT BEINGS AVAILABLE FOR ASSISTANCE. HOW OPEN ARE YOU TO THE CONCEPT OF CALLING UPON LIGHT BEINGS FOR GUIDANCE?

_____
_____
_____
_____

WHAT KIND OF QUESTIONS WOULD YOU LIKE TO POSE TO THE LIGHT BEINGS IN YOUR SPIRITUAL PRACTICE?

_____
_____
_____
_____

I listen to SPIRIT

HOW CAN YOU HELP TO ESTABLISH A CLEARER LINE OF COMMUNICATION?

ARE THERE SPECIFIC EMOTIONS OR FEELINGS YOU WANT TO BRING INTO YOUR INTERACTIONS?

ARE THERE SPECIFIC EMOTIONS OR FEELINGS YOU WANT TO BRING INTO YOUR INTERACTIONS?

AM I ABLE TO HEAR THE QUIET VOICE OF SPIRIT? WAYS TO BUILD THAT TRUST.

WEEKLY PROGRESS / NOTABLE EXPERIENCES

Gyla

Growth, Expansion and Creativity

Use Gyla in meditation to access greater levels of creativity or creation. It can also aid in growth, expansion, or development. Gently gaze upon Gyla with soft eyes and trust the creative flow.

HOW DO YOU DEFINE CREATIVITY, AND HOW DOES IT MANIFEST IN YOUR LIFE? CAN YOU CREATIVELY GIVE GRATITUDE FOR CIRCUMSTANCES THAT ARISE?

_____
_____
_____
_____

GYLA SHOWS YOU A BEAUTIFUL WAY TO WALK YOUR PATH, ARE YOU ABLE TO POSITIVELY UNDERSTAND SOUL LESSONS IN THESE CIRCUMSTANCES AS THE PIECES OF YOUR LIFE FALL INTO PLACE?

_____
_____
_____
_____

I am CREATION

WHAT CAN YOU DO TO REMIND YOURSELF OF THE LESSONS OF LIFE AND STAY IN A POSITIVE MID SET?

HOW CAN YOU SEE THE BEAUTY AMONGST THE CHAOS?

HOW CAN I SEE MY DIVINE PATH AMONGST THE CHAOS?

WHAT HAPPENS WHEN I LET GO AND TRUST IN MY DIVINE PATH?

WEEKLY PROGRESS / NOTABLE EXPERIENCES

Kahli

Karma

All experiences contribute to our soul's growth. Our choices and interactions create our karma. Kahli symbolizes the release of karma. No lesson is a mistake; all are opportunities to learn and evolve. Let Kahli guide you through releasing any karmic lessons you're ready to let go of.

WHEN TURMOIL OCCURS IN YOUR LIFE, ARE YOU ABLE TO LET GO OF THE NEED TO KNOW "WHY WE ARE THE WAY WE ARE"

_____
_____
_____
_____

DO YOU FIXATE ON CIRCUMSTANCES BEING CAUSED BY PAST LIVES?

_____
_____
_____
_____

I am
PRESENT

I BRING MYSELF BACK TO THE PRESENT MOMENT WHEN?

_____
_____
_____
_____
_____
_____
_____
_____
_____
_____

WHAT KARMIC TIES ARE READY TO BE RELEASED?

_____
_____
_____
_____
_____
_____

AS KARMA CLEARS, WHERE DO I NOTICE THE DIFFERENCE IN MY EMOTIONS?

_____
_____
_____
_____
_____
_____

WEEKLY PROGRESS / NOTABLE EXPERIENCES

Ughma

Connection to Soul, Soul Retrieval, Authentic Self

Ughma guides us to reclaim our authenticity by integrating fragmented pieces of our love through truth, trust, and releasing that which doesn't belong to us. We are whole and always have been, and Ughma reminds us to let go of the lack of love and embrace our true selves.

WHAT ASPECTS OF EXPERIENCE CONTRIBUTE TO YOUR SENSE OF AUTHENTICITY?

_____
_____
_____
_____
_____

WHAT EXPERIENCES OR BELIEFS HAVE CONTRIBUTED TO A SENSE OF FRAGMENTATION?

_____
_____
_____
_____
_____

HOW CAN YOU RECLAIM A SENSE OF WHOLENESS BY RELEASING WHAT NO LONGER SERVES YOU?

WHAT SPECIFIC QUALITIES OR ASPECTS OF YOURSELF WOULD YOU SEEK TO RECLAIM?

- [ ]
- [ ]
- [ ]
- [ ]
- [ ]
- [ ]
- [ ]

HOW CAN YOU FOSTER A MORE COMPLETE AND AUTHENTIC EXPRESSION OF SELF?

- [ ]
- [ ]
- [ ]
- [ ]
- [ ]
- [ ]
- [ ]

"Embrace truth, trust, integrate, become whole."
~LAARA

WEEKLY PROGRESS / NOTABLE EXPERIENCES

Suri brings comfort and grounding to ease your struggles and help you gather more light. It creates a space for you to reach deep within yourself and connect with pure joy and understanding beyond your limited senses.

HOW CAN YOU ACTIVELY SEEK AND CULTIVATE MORE OF THIS LIGHT IN YOUR DAILY LIFE?

_____
_____
_____
_____
_____

WHAT STEPS CAN YOU TAKE TO EASE THE STRUGGLES AND CREATE SPACE FOR MORE LIGHT TO ENTER?

_____
_____
_____
_____

I am ENLIGHTENED

ENVISION A PLACE OF PURE LIGHT AND JOY WITHIN YOURSELF. WHAT DOES THIS PLACE LOOK AND FEEL LIKE?

WHAT PRACTICES OR ACTIVITIES HELP YOU CONNECT TO THIS INNER STILLNESS?

HOW MIGHT EMBRACING SURI'S ENERGY SUPPORT IN GAINING A SENSE OF OPENNESS AND ACCEPTANCE?

WEEKLY PROGRESS / NOTABLE EXPERIENCES

Commagt symbolizes the release of confusion that blocks our ability to see clearly and leads to struggle. It helps us let go of false stories and conclusions created by our conscious ego mind. Use it to clear confusion about relationships, jobs, situations, or bigger concepts like the interconnectedness of all things.

HOW CAN YOU RELEASE FALSE STORIES OR CONCLUSIONS CREATED BY YOUR CONSCIOUS EGO?

_____
_____
_____
_____

HOW HAVE THESE STORIES CONTRIBUTED TO STRUGGLES IN YOUR LIFE?

_____
_____
_____
_____

I am MYSELF

IN WHAT WAYS HAS CONFUSION AFFECTED YOUR PROFESSIONAL LIFE?

_____
_____
_____
_____
_____
_____
_____
_____
_____
_____

HOW CAN I GAIN A CLEARER PERSPECTIVE ON THESE CIRCUMSTANCES?

_____
_____
_____
_____
_____
_____

WHAT PRACTICES ASSIST IN GAINING A BETTER UNDERSTANDING?

_____
_____
_____
_____
_____
_____
_____

WEEKLY PROGRESS / NOTABLE EXPERIENCES

Zahay'kma

Forgiving Self

Forgiveness is recognizing self and others as Divine Beings of Love, fellow travelers on a karmic path. It's about releasing misguided perceptions, embracing innocence, and finding positive intent in situations. By letting go of judgment, we create space for growth and self-discovery, fostering a path to inner peace and understanding.

HOW DOES VIEWING YOURSELF AND OTHERS AS DIVINE BEINGS OF LOVE CONTRIBUTE TO YOUR HEALING?

_____
_____
_____
_____

HOW MIGHT RECOGNIZING DIVINITY IN YOURSELF SHIFT YOUR PERSPECTIVE?

_____
_____
_____
_____

I FORGIVE

HOW HAS FORGIVENESS CONTRIBUTED TO YOUR PERSONAL JOURNEY OF SELF-DISCOVERY AND GROWTH?

HOW HAS FORGIVENESS FOSTERED A SENSE OF OPENNESS TO NEW EXPERIENCES?

HOW CAN FORGIVENESS RELEASE JUDGMENT?

HOW CAN FORGIVENESS GUIDE YOU IN SEEKING THE POSITIVE ASPECTS AND LESSONS?

WEEKLY PROGRESS / NOTABLE EXPERIENCES

Anami is a symbol that connects you with your Heart. Place a hand over your Heart and set the intention to work with Anami's energies. Inhale and feel the intensity grow. Sit with Anami for as long as you feel is necessary.

AS YOU PLACE YOUR HAND OVER YOUR HEART TO WORK WITH ANAMI'S ENERGIES, WHAT SENSATIONS, THOUGHTS, OR EMOTIONS ARISE DURING THIS INITIAL CONNECTION?

_____
_____
_____
_____
_____

HOW CAN YOU DEEPEN YOUR UNDERSTANDING OF THE HEART'S SYMBOLIC AND ENERGETIC IMPORTANCE?

_____
_____
_____
_____
_____

I love MYSELF

HOW DOES CONNECTING WITH ANAMI DEEPEN YOUR UNDERSTANDING OF HEART?

HOW DOES IT'S SOFT INTENSITY MANIFEST IN YOUR BODY,

HOW DOES THIS SENSE OF SOLIDITY IMPACT YOUR PERCEPTION OF SELF?

ARE THERE SPECIFIC INSIGHTS OR REALIZATIONS THAT EMERGE?

ADD A LITTLE BIT OF BODY TEXT

The Love That You Are

Self-Love, Knowing One's Worth, Expression of Self

Identifying one another through the signature of Love, a unique expression within the whole, reveals individuality. This symbol guides the discovery of inner Love, enhancing a more connected and integrated self. Spend 15-20 minutes in quiet reflection, deepening your connection to the Heart Center, allowing it to expand into space.

DESCRIBE THE SENSATIONS AND EMOTIONS THAT ARISE DURING THIS CONNECTION.

_____
_____
_____
_____

HOW DOES THIS CONNECTION ENHANCE YOUR AWARENESS OF YOUR OWN LOVE SIGNATURE?

_____
_____
_____
_____

I am
LOVE

QUALITIES THAT MAKE UP YOUR PERSONAL LOVE SIGNATURE?

_____
_____
_____
_____
_____
_____
_____
_____
_____

HOW DOES THE SYMBOL RESONATE WITH YOU?

_____
_____
_____
_____
_____
_____

HOW CAN YOU ENHANCE YOUR SELF-EXPRESSION?

_____
_____
_____
_____
_____
_____
_____

WEEKLY PROGRESS / NOTABLE EXPERIENCES

Jyak'ma

Self-Reflection, Self-Discovery, Self-Exploration

Jyak'ma involves profound self-awareness, exploring and embracing our essence. Through self-discovery, we engage with our gifts, participating in the world consciously. Incarnating on Earth, we choose to interact with specific karma. Our developed personality becomes a temporary "mask" in life's play, offering opportunities for growth and expansion.

HOW DO THESE GIFTS CONTRIBUTE TO YOUR ABILITY TO PARTICIPATE IN THE WORLD WITH SELF-AWARENESS?

HOW HAS EXPLORING, DISCOVERING, AND REFLECTING SHAPED YOUR SELF-UNDERSTANDING?

REFLECT ON POSSIBLE KARMIC INTERACTIONS. ARE THERE ANY PATTERNS? HOW DO THEY CONTRIBUTE TO PERSONAL GROWTH AND EVOLUTION?

HOW HAS YOUR PERSONALITY DEVELOPED THROUGHOUT YOUR LIFE?	HOW DOES VIEWING LIFE AS A PLAY HELP NAVIGATE CHALLENGES WITH LEARNING INSIGHT?
☐ _____	☐ _____
☐ _____	☐ _____
☐ _____	☐ _____
☐ _____	☐ _____
☐ _____	☐ _____
☐ _____	☐ _____
☐ _____	☐ _____

"Embrace, explore, reflect; self-awareness unfolds."
~LAARA

WEEKLY PROGRESS / NOTABLE EXPERIENCES

Galagma prompts embracing your excellence as a Divine Being of Love. Discard self-imposed limits and engage with the energy flow. Encourages continual spiritual exploration through practices like meditation, writing, or yoga. You are never alone; ask, and supportive beings of Light are ready to guide you.

REFLECT ON THE IDEA OF CALLING FORTH YOUR EXCELLENCE. WHAT DOES EXCELLENCE MEAN TO YOU IN THE CONTEXT OF YOUR LIFE AND ENDEAVORS?

_____
_____
_____
_____
_____

HOW CAN YOU ACTIVELY SUMMON AND EXPRESS YOUR DIVINE QUALITIES IN YOUR DAILY ACTIONS AND INTERACTIONS?

_____
_____
_____
_____
_____

I love from WITHIN

WHAT BELIEFS OR HABITS ARE HOLDING YOU BACK?

_____
_____
_____
_____
_____
_____
_____
_____
_____
_____

HOW CAN YOU OPEN YOURSELF TO THE BOUNDLESS POTENTIAL THAT LIES WITHIN YOU?

_____
_____
_____
_____
_____
_____

IN WHAT WAYS CAN YOU STRENGTHEN YOUR CONNECTION TO KUNDALINI ENERGY?

_____
_____
_____
_____
_____
_____

WEEKLY PROGRESS / NOTABLE EXPERIENCES

Tungah

Aligning with Information

This symbol, Tungah, helps us to take any concept we are struggling with understanding, learning, or integrating, and assists us in bridging the gap. It can help us to remove blocks we may hold, to move past a language barrier, or to be open to receiving new information.

WHAT BELIEFS OR PRECONCEPTIONS MIGHT BE HINDERING YOUR ABILITY TO GRASP NEW INFORMATION?

_____
_____
_____
_____

HOW CAN YOU REMOVE THESE BLOCKS AND FOSTER A MORE OPEN AND RECEPTIVE MINDSET?

_____
_____
_____
_____

I am ALIGNED

WHAT STEPS CAN YOU TAKE TO BE MORE OPEN TO RECEIVING INFORMATION?

_____
_____
_____
_____
_____
_____
_____
_____
_____
_____

ARE THERE AREAS IN YOUR LIFE WHERE YOU MAY BE RESISTANT TO LEARNING OR INTEGRATING NEW CONCEPTS?

_____
_____
_____
_____
_____

HOW MIGHT TUNGAH ASSIST YOU IN BRIDGING THE GAP AND MOVING BEYOND THESE STRUGGLES?

_____
_____
_____
_____
_____
_____

WEEKLY PROGRESS / NOTABLE EXPERIENCES

Kalak'tuk

Integrating Dimensions,
Moving through Dimensions,
Collapsing Time

This symbol, Kalak'tuk, introduces the idea that we human beings have the capacity to work with time in a more masterful way. Why take years or lifetimes to heal, for example, when we could collapse time and heal in days, hours, or minutes? Kalak'tuk is showing us this potential, opening our awareness to this reality.

HOW DO YOU TYPICALLY APPROACH THE PASSAGE OF TIME, ESPECIALLY IN RELATION TO PERSONAL GROWTH AND HEALING?

_____
_____
_____
_____
_____

IN WHAT WAYS CAN YOU ENVISION WORKING WITH TIME MORE MASTERFULLY?

_____
_____
_____
_____
_____

I am TIMELESS

HOW MIGHT THE CONCEPT OF COLLAPSING TIME RESONATE WITH YOUR HEALING JOURNEY?

WHAT BELIEFS OR LIMITATIONS ABOUT TIME CAN YOU RELEASE?

_____
_____
_____
_____
_____

HOW CAN YOU OPEN YOUR AWARENESS TO VARIOUS ASPECTS OF YOUR LIFE, BEYOND HEALING?

_____
_____
_____
_____
_____

HOW CAN FORGIVENESS GUIDE YOU IN SEEKING THE POSITIVE ASPECTS AND LESSONS?

_____
_____
_____
_____
_____

WEEKLY PROGRESS / NOTABLE EXPERIENCES

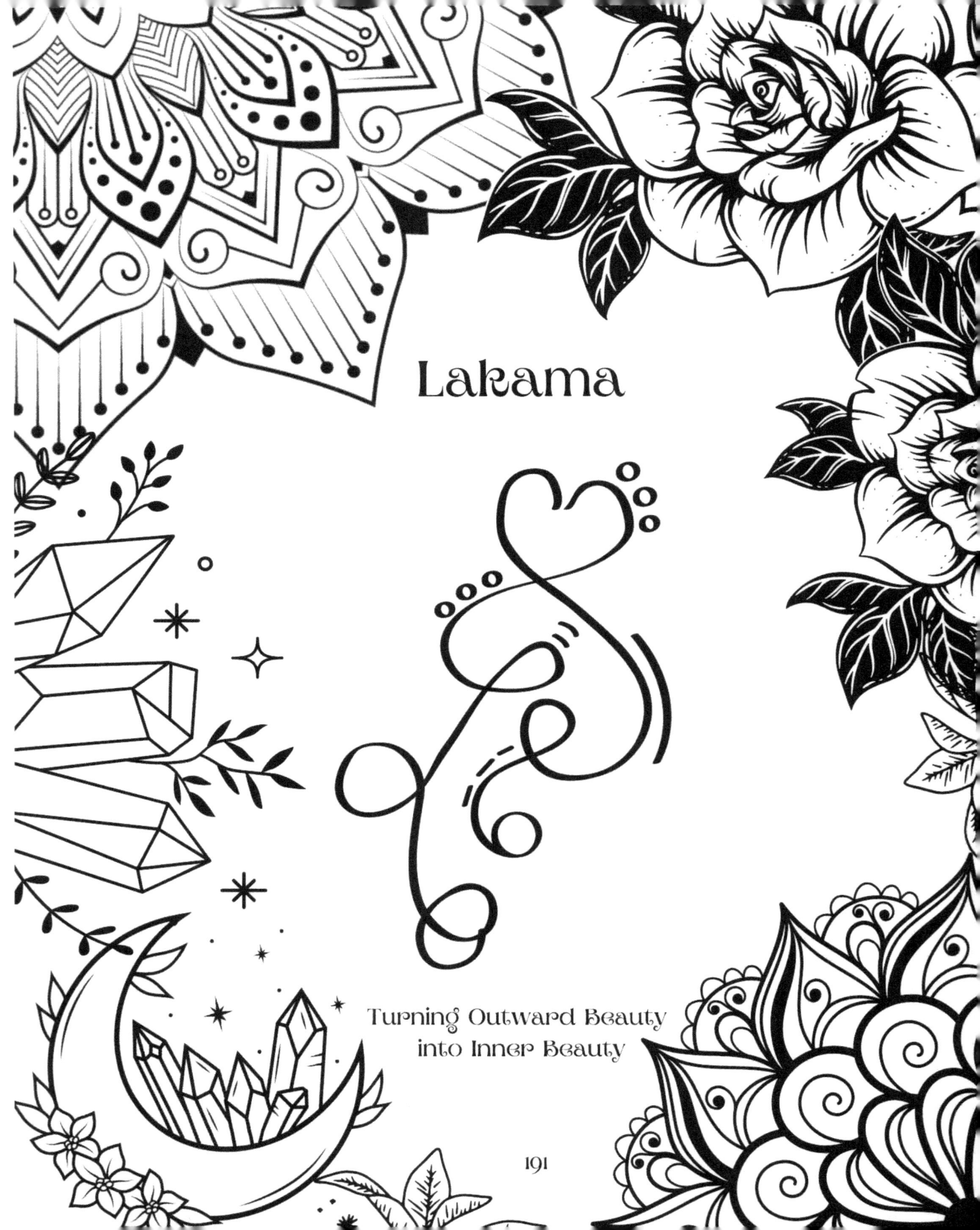

Lakama

Turning Outward Beauty into Inner Beauty

Many of us are guilty of projecting our desire for Love upon someone or something other than ourselves. We hope that actively loving another person will relieve the pain of not loving ourselves. Kakama invites you to bring more of your Love forward, and offer it to yourself.

WHAT ARE SOME EXAMPLES OF SITUATIONS WHERE YOU SOUGHT EXTERNAL SOURCES OF LOVE TO FILL A VOID WITHIN YOURSELF?

_____
_____
_____
_____

HOW HAS THE LACK OF SELF-LOVE MANIFESTED IN YOUR LIFE?

_____
_____
_____
_____

I love MYSELF

IN WHAT WAYS DO YOU SEEK RELIEF THROUGH EXTERNAL SOURCES?

WHAT ACTIVITIES BRING YOU JOY, PEACE, AND A SENSE OF FULFILLMENT?

___

___

___

___

HOW CAN YOU REDIRECT YOUR ENERGY TOWARDS SELF-NURTURING?

___

___

___

___

WHAT STEPS CAN YOU TAKE TO MAKE SELF-LOVE A PRIORITY IN YOUR LIFE?

___

___

___

___

WEEKLY PROGRESS / NOTABLE EXPERIENCES

Shizama

Releasing Negative Energy Space

This symbol works in two ways to assist us in releasing negative energy space. We need to make sure our homes are free of lower vibrational energy so our environment will help us in our healing journey. Shizama will help you to release negative energy within and around you.

TAKE A MOMENT TO ASSESS THE ENERGY IN YOUR HOME. HOW WOULD YOU DESCRIBE THE OVERALL VIBE OR ATMOSPHERE?

_____
_____
_____
_____

REFLECT ON SITUATIONS OR EXPERIENCES THAT MAY TRIGGER NEGATIVE ENERGY WITHIN YOU. WHAT PATTERNS OR EVENTS TEND TO BRING ABOUT LOWER VIBRATIONAL FEELINGS?

_____
_____
_____
_____

I am
PURE

WHAT STEPS CAN YOU TAKE TO ENSURE YOUR HOME IS FREE OF LOWER VIBRATIONAL ENERGY?

_____
_____
_____
_____
_____
_____
_____
_____
_____

HOW CAN YOU CONFRONT AND RELEASE TRIGGERS FOR A HARMONIOUS INTERNAL ENVIRONMENT?

_____
_____
_____
_____
_____
_____

HOW CAN YOU RELEASE NEGATIVE ENERGY WITHIN AND AROUND YOU?

_____
_____
_____
_____
_____
_____
_____

WEEKLY PROGRESS / NOTABLE EXPERIENCES

Jayagk

Release Toxins on All Levels

During contemplation and meditation, use this symbol to address toxic energies. Choose to release toxins, seeking assistance from Jayagk. With clear intentions, envision the transmutation of unwanted energies. Stay with the release process. After completion, ask Jayagk to fill the spaces with Light, feeling its warmth and purity. Express gratitude for Jayagk's assistance.

WHAT SITUATIONS OR RELATIONSHIPS CONTRIBUTE TO FEELINGS OF NEGATIVITY OR TOXICITY? TAKE SOME TIME TO IDENTIFY AND ACKNOWLEDGE THESE ELEMENTS.

_____

_____

_____

_____

WHAT SPECIFIC NEGATIVE PATTERNS, EMOTIONS, OR SITUATIONS DO YOU WISH TO LET GO OF?

_____

_____

_____

_____

DURING MEDITATION, ENVISION THE RELEASE AND TRANSMUTATION OF THE TOXIC ENERGIES YOU IDENTIFIED. WHAT DOES THIS PROCESS LOOK AND FEEL LIKE?

WHAT SENSATIONS OR EMOTIONS ARISE AS YOU LET GO OF THESE TOXIC ENERGIES?

- [ ] _____
- [ ] _____
- [ ] _____
- [ ] _____
- [ ] _____
- [ ] _____
- [ ] _____

HOW DOES IT FEEL TO CONSCIOUSLY RELEASE AND CREATE SPACE FOR RENEWAL WITHIN YOURSELF?

- [ ] _____
- [ ] _____
- [ ] _____
- [ ] _____
- [ ] _____
- [ ] _____

"Release toxins, embrace Light's purity, gratitude to Jayagk."

~LAARA

WEEKLY PROGRESS / NOTABLE EXPERIENCES

Panma

Moving with Light, Expanding Frequencies

Panma guides us to embrace a greater spectrum of Light, dancing in unlimited joy. In quantum physics, light behaves as both particle and wave. In our spiritual journey, we navigate between being a particle and a wave, experiencing the duality of our existence.

REFLECT ON YOUR CURRENT ABILITY TO HOLD AND EMBODY LIGHT. HOW WOULD YOU DESCRIBE THE RANGE OF FREQUENCIES YOU ARE COMFORTABLE WITH?

_____
_____
_____
_____

EXPANDING YOUR ABILITY TO HOLD MORE LIGHT WITH UNLIMITED JOY. WHAT DOES JOY IN THE CONTEXT OF WORKING WITH LIGHT MEAN TO YOU?

_____
_____
_____
_____

I grow from LIGHT

HOW CAN YOU ADD MORE JOY INTO YOUR SPIRITUAL PRACTICES?

_____
_____
_____
_____
_____
_____
_____
_____
_____
_____

HOW CAN YOU ADD MORE PLAYFULNESS INTO YOUR SPIRITUAL JOURNEY?

_____
_____
_____
_____
_____

WHAT EMOTIONS OR SENSATIONS ACCOMPANY THESE DIFFERENT STATES OF BEING?

_____
_____
_____
_____
_____
_____
_____

WEEKLY PROGRESS / NOTABLE EXPERIENCES

Kalimar helps us find oneness and soul family connection. Letting go of what's not ours frees what is meant to be, leading to a deeper experience of unity.

REFLECT ON YOUR UNDERSTANDING OF THE FREQUENCY OF ONENESS. WHAT DOES ONENESS MEAN TO YOU IN THE CONTEXT OF SOUL FAMILY CONNECTION?

_____
_____
_____
_____

HOW CAN YOU APPROACH THE JOURNEY OF SOUL FAMILY CONNECTION WITH A SENSE OF OPENNESS AND SURRENDER?

_____
_____
_____
_____

I am DIVINITY

WHAT INNATE QUALITIES OF YOURSELF DO YOU NEED TO LIBERATE AND ALLOW TO COME FORWARD?

_____
_____
_____
_____
_____
_____
_____
_____
_____
_____

IN WHAT WAYS DOES SURRENDERING CONTRIBUTE TO A SENSE OF ONENESS AND UNITY?

_____
_____
_____
_____
_____
_____

HOW CAN YOU STRENGTHEN YOUR CONNECTION TO THE FREQUENCY OF ONENESS AND SOUL FAMILY?

_____
_____
_____
_____
_____
_____
_____

WEEKLY PROGRESS / NOTABLE EXPERIENCES

Our souls yearn for growth and expansion, joyfully exploring life's experiences. Through dance and play, we navigate our journey, doing inner healing to find ease within life's lessons, heal fears, and embrace limitless love. I AM. The I AM Presence is our whole, complete, knowing essence. We are Love.

REFLECT ON YOUR SOUL'S INNATE DESIRE FOR GROWTH AND EXPANSION. WHAT ASPECTS OF YOUR LIFE CURRENTLY ALIGN WITH THIS DESIRE?

___

___

___

___

IN WHAT WAYS CAN YOU FOSTER A MINDSET OF CURIOSITY AND OPENNESS TO EXPERIENCE FOR THE PURPOSE OF SOULFUL EXPLORATION?

___

___

___

___

I am all
THAT I AM

WHAT FEARS OR LIMITATIONS ARE YOU CURRENTLY WORKING THROUGH?

REFLECT ON MOMENTS WHEN YOU HAVE FELT WHOLE, COMPLETE, AND KNOWING.

HOW CAN YOU ALIGN MORE CONSCIOUSLY WITH YOUR I AM PRESENCE IN YOUR DAILY LIFE?

HOW CAN YOU EMBODY AND RADIATE LOVE IN VARIOUS ASPECTS OF YOUR LIFE?

WEEKLY PROGRESS / NOTABLE EXPERIENCES

Congratulations!

Congratulations on completing *The Little Book of Light Codes Workbook*! Not only have you taken the time to experience what each of the 52 Light Codes have to offer, but you also reflected upon deep aspects of ourself that required bravery and honesty. This is deep work that you will hopefully receive benefits from as you continue to evolve on your incredible path.

If you haven't already, be sure to check out our sequel, The Little Book of Light Codes Volume 2: Ascension Codes. This is the next step on our Light Codes journey to awakening and advancement.

Thank you for including these sacred codes on your ascension path.

Wishing you happiness, health and abundance with all my Love,

Laara

www.ingramcontent.com/pod-product-compliance
Lightning Source LLC
Chambersburg PA
CBHW042357070526
44585CB00029B/2969